THE COOKOUT COOKBOOK

Compiled by Judith Ferguson
Tested and prepared by Jacqueline Bellefontaine

CLB1505
© 1987 Colour Library Books Ltd., Godalming, Surrey, England
All rights reserved
This edition published in 1993 by SMITHMARK Publishers Inc.,
16 East 32nd Street, New York, NY 10016
SMITHMARK books are available for bulk purchase for sales promotion
and premium use. For details write or call the manager of special sales,
SMITHMARK Publishers Inc., 16 East 32nd Street,
New York, NY 10016; (212) 532-6600.
ISBN 0-8317-1764-5
Printed in Singapore

THE COOKOUT
COOKBOOK

SMITHMARK

CONTENTS

Before gas and electricity were harnessed for our cooking convenience, our ancestors employed barbecue cooking, although they didn't know it by that name. Flaming food, however, seemed to go out of fashion for a time in northern Europe, except in chafing dishes in expensive restaurants. Countries with sunnier climates kept up the art and the United States, where informality is the spirit of entertaining, adopted barbecue cooking as its own.

A barbecue grill can be a very primitive arrangement of a firebowl – a place to hold charcoal or wood – and a rack, or some support to hold the food. Modern design has added several different interpretations:

Portable barbecue grills – These are small and are often called picnic barbecues. They have folding or telescopic legs. Table-top models with short legs and hibachis in various sizes are popular styles.

Semi-portable grills – These are slightly larger and have fixed legs, sometimes with wheels for easy movement. They are often round with rotating racks, good for moving food quickly off hot-spots, or adjustable shelves. Rotisseries can be fixed to these grills and most have windshields along the back.

Hooded grills – These keep the food at an even temperature and the smoke out of the cook's eyes! With practice, whole meals can be cooked, and food can be smoked over aromatic wood chips for extra flavour.

Home-made grills – Barbecues can be built of brick or stone with oven shelves for racks.

Electric and gas grills – These use special rocks that radiate heat from electric coils or gas flames. They give the taste and appearance of charcoal-grilled food along with control over the intensity of heat. A dial with a number of settings allows more delicate foods to be cooked through without charring on the outside. These grills are cleaner and heat much faster than charcoal or wood-fired grills, which must be lit at least 1 hour before cooking. They are also nearly self-cleaning. The recipes in this book were cooked on an electric grill from Redring Electric Company.

When choosing a fuel for barbecueing, you should bear in mind that charcoal compressed into briquettes will burn for twice as long with more uniform heat than lumpwood charcoal – irregular-sized pieces of kiln-charred hardwood. However, lumpwood charcoal is easier to light than briquettes. Vine wood cuttings are an alternative to charcoal, but do not burn as long. Hardwood, such as birch or cherry can be used, but takes a long time to light and is expensive.

Firelighters, either liquid or solid, get the fire going faster. Use them to start a fire, but never, for safety reasons, on coals that are already hot. With any grill that uses charcoal or wood, be sure the fire bowl has perforations in the bottom and sides, or that the coals can sit on a perforated rack inside. This allows air to circulate underneath and makes the fire easier to light and keep going.

Special equipment is not necessary, but long-handled cooking utensils are easiest and safest to use. When grilling fish, a hinged wire rack, specially shaped for both small or large fish, is a great help. So, too, are square hinged racks for turning a number of hamburgers, sausages or steaks at the same time.

Cooking times for barbecued food cannot be very exact. There is room for variation depending on the type of grill and source of heat. For grills without adjustable shelves, results are better if the food is cooked in the oven for about half to three-quarters of the cooking time and the remaining time on the barbecue grill for colour and flavour. Similarly, larger cuts of meat, such as Butterflied Lamb, will cook faster and be juicer if pre-cooked in the oven. In fact, employ this method with any food cooked for a large group and you will avoid the problem of eating in shifts.

Salads are a natural accompaniment to barbecued food. On a warm summer's day or evening they can also be a light and refreshing meal in themselves. So when summer arrives, abandon your oven occasionally and try barbecues and salads and discover why food tastes so much better when cooked and eaten outdoors.

THE COOKOUT COOKBOOK

APPETIZERS AND SIDE SALADS

Satay

PREPARATION TIME:	25 minutes
COOKING TIME:	10-15 minutes
SERVES:	4 people

1lb chicken, skinned, boned and cut into 1 inch cubes

MARINADE
2 tbsps soy sauce
2 tbsps oil
2 tbsps lime juice
1 tsp ground cumin
1 tsp turmeric
2 tsps ground coriander

SAUCE
2 tbsps oil
1 small onion, finely chopped
1 tsp chili powder
1 cup peanut butter
1 tsp brown sugar
Remaining marinade

GARNISH
Lime wedges
Coriander leaves

Combine the marinade ingredients in a deep bowl. Put in the meat and stir to coat. Leave covered in the refrigerator for 1 hour. Drain and thread the meat on 4 large or 8 small skewers. Grill about 10-15 minutes, turning frequently to cook all sides. Baste often. Meanwhile heat the oil in a small saucepan. Add the onion and the chili powder. Cook until the onion is slightly softened. Remove from the heat and set aside. When the meat is nearly cooked combine the marinade with the oil and onion and chili powder. Stir in the remaining sauce ingredients, thinning with water if necessary. Brush the Satay with the sauce 1-2 minutes before the end of cooking time. Spoon over a bit more sauce and serve the rest separately. Garnish each serving with lime wedges and

This page: **Rumaki (left) and Satay (right). Facing page: Grilled Garlic Shrimp (left) and Smoked Fish Kebabs with Horseradish Sauce (right).**

coriander leaves.

Rumaki

PREPARATION TIME: 15 minutes	
COOKING TIME: 10-15 minutes	
SERVES: 4 people	

¾ cup soy sauce
1lb chicken livers, trimmed and cut into 2
    inch pieces
1 7oz can water chestnuts, drained
8 slices smoked streaky bacon
1 red pepper, cut in 1 inch pieces
Brown sugar

Combine half the soy sauce and all the chicken livers in a deep bowl. Leave to marinate in the refrigerator for 1 hour. Place the bacon slices on a wooden board. Stretch the bacon by running the back of a knife backwards and forwards over each slice. Cut the slices in half across. Drain the chicken livers and discard the soy sauce. Put a piece of liver and a water chestnut on each slice of bacon and roll up. Thread onto skewers, alternating with a piece of red pepper. Grill on an oiled rack above hot coals for 10-15 minutes, basting with the remaining half of the soy sauce and turning frequently. One minute before the end of cooking, sprinkle lightly with brown sugar and allow to glaze. Garnish serving dishes with parsley if desired.

Greek Salad

PREPARATION TIME: 15 minutes	
SERVES: 4 people	

1 head romaine lettuce
16 black olives, stoned
1 cup crumbled feta cheese
1 small can anchovies, drained
8 mild pickled peppers
2oz cherry tomatoes, halved
½ cucumber, cut in small dice
2 tbsps chopped fresh oregano or 1 tbsp
    dried oregano

DRESSING
½ cup olive oil
3 tbsps red wine vinegar
1 clove garlic, finely minced
Salt and pepper

Wash and dry the romaine lettuce and tear the leaves into bite-size pieces. Place the leaves in a large salad bowl and arrange or scatter all the other ingredients on top of the lettuce. If the anchovies are large, cut them into thinner strips or chop into small pieces. Sprinkle the fresh or dried oregano over all the ingredients in the salad bowl. Mix the dressing together well and pour over the salad just before serving.

Caesar Salad

PREPARATION TIME: 20 minutes	
COOKING TIME: 3 minutes	
SERVES: 4-6 people	

1 large or two small heads romaine lettuce
8 slices white bread, crusts removed
½ cup oil
1 clove garlic, peeled
1 small can anchovies
3oz fresh Parmesan cheese

DRESSING
1 egg
½ cup olive oil
Juice of 1 lemon
1 clove garlic, finely minced
Salt and pepper

Wash the lettuce and dry well. Tear the lettuce into bite-size pieces and place in a large salad bowl, or four individual bowls. Cut the slices of bread into ½ inch dice. Heat the vegetable oil in a small frying pan. When the oil is hot put in the clove of garlic and the cubes of bread. Lower the heat slightly and, using a metal spoon, keep stirring the cubes of bread to brown them evenly. When they are golden brown and crisp, remove them to paper towels to drain. Add the anchovies to the lettuce in the salad bowl and sprinkle on the fried bread croûtons. To prepare the dressing, place the egg in boiling water for 1 minute. Break into a small bowl and combine with remaining dressing ingredients, whisking very well. Pour the dressing over the salad and toss. Using a cheese slicer, shave off thin slices of Parmesan cheese and add to the salad. Alternatively, grate the cheese and add to the salad with the dressing.

Smoked Fish Kebabs with Horseradish Sauce

PREPARATION TIME: 15 minutes	
COOKING TIME: 6 minutes	
SERVES: 4 people	

1 smoked kipper fillet, skinned and cut
    into 1 inch pieces
1 smoked haddock fillet, skinned and cut
    into 1 inch pieces
8 bay leaves
1 small red onion, quartered
Oil

SAUCE
2 tbsps grated fresh or bottled horseradish
1 cup sour cream
2 tsps fresh dill, chopped
Salt and pepper
Squeeze of lemon juice
Pinch sugar

Thread the fish, bay leaves and slices of onion on skewers, alternating ingredients and types of fish. Brush with oil and place on an oiled grill rack above hot coals. Mix the sauce ingredients together and divide onto side plates. Grill the kebabs for about 6 minutes, turning and basting with oil frequently. When the onion is cooked, remove to serving dishes. Place kebabs on lettuce leaves, if desired, for serving.

Grilled Garlic Shrimp

PREPARATION TIME: 15 minutes	
COOKING TIME: 8-10 minutes	
SERVES: 4 people	

2lbs uncooked jumbo shrimp
4 tbsps melted butter

Facing page: Greek Salad (top) and Caesar Salad (bottom).

MARINADE
3 cloves garlic, finely chopped
4 tbsps oil
½ cup lemon juice
4 tbsps chopped basil
Salt
Coarsely ground black pepper

Shell and de-vein the shrimp. Leave the shell on the ends of the tails. Combine the marinade ingredients in a plastic bag. Put in the shrimp and seal the bag. Refrigerate for 1 hour, turning frequently. Place the bag in a bowl to catch possible drips. Drain the shrimp and thread onto 4 skewers. Mix the marinade with the melted butter and brush the shrimp with the mixture. Grill for 8-10 minutes about 4-6 inches above the coals. Brush frequently with the

marinade while the shrimp cook. Pour over remaining marinade before serving.

Carrot Salad with Creamy Sesame Dressing

PREPARATION TIME: 1 hour

SERVES: 4 people

4 large carrots, peeled
1 cup raisins
1 cup chopped walnuts
2 tbsps sesame seeds
2 tbsps oil
1 tbsp lemon juice
6 tbsps sesame paste (tahini)
6 tbsps warm water

2 tbsps heavy cream
Salt and pepper
1 tbsp sugar

Place the carrots in iced water for 1 hour. Dry them and grate coarsely into a bowl. Add the raisins, nuts and sesame seeds. Mix the dressing ingredients together, adding more cream if the dressing appears too thick. If dressing separates, whisk vigorously until it comes together before adding additional cream. Toss with the carrot salad and serve.

Curried Rice Salad

PREPARATION TIME: 20 minutes

COOKING TIME: 12 minutes

SERVES: 6 people

¾ cup long grain rice
1 tbsp curry powder, hot or mild as desired
4 green onions, sliced
2 sticks celery, sliced
1 small green pepper, diced
10 black olives, halved and stoned
¼ cup golden raisins
¼ cup toasted sliced almonds
4 tbsps flaked coconut
2 hard-boiled eggs, chopped

DRESSING
½ cup mayonnaise
1 tbsp mango chutney
Juice and grated rind of ½ a lime
4 tbsps natural yogurt
Salt

GARNISH
2 avocados, peeled and cut in cubes
Juice of ½ lemon or lime

Cook the rice in boiling salted water for about 12 minutes or until tender. During the last 3 minutes of cooking time drain away half the water and stir in the curry powder. Leave to continue cooking over a gentle heat until the rice is cooked and the water is evaporated. Leave covered to stand for about 5 minutes. Toss the

This page: Carrot Salad with Creamy Sesame Dressing. Facing page: Curried Rice Salad.

rice with a fork, drain away any excess water and leave to cool. Combine with the remaining salad ingredients, stirring carefully so that the hard-boiled eggs do not break up. Mix the dressing ingredients together thoroughly. Chop any large pieces of mango in the chutney finely. Stir the dressing into the salad and toss gently to coat. Arrange the rice salad in a mound on a serving dish. Sprinkle the cubed avocado with the lemon juice to keep it green and place around the rice salad before serving.

Cheese and Vine Leaves

PREPARATION TIME: 20 minutes

COOKING TIME: 6 minutes

SERVES: 4 people

4 pieces goat's, feta or haloumi cheese
1 cup olive oil
4 tbsps chopped fresh herbs such as basil,
  tarragon, oregano, marjoram, parsley
2 cloves garlic, peeled and crushed
  (optional)
1 bay leaf
Squeeze lemon juice

TO SERVE
4 fresh vine leaves, washed, or 4 brine-
  packed vine leaves, soaked 30 minutes
1 head radicchio
8 leaves curly endive, washed and torn in
  bite-size pieces

If using goat's cheese, make sure it is not too ripe. Lightly score the surface of whichever cheese is used. Mix together the oil, herbs, garlic and lemon juice. Place the cheese in a small, deep bowl or jar and pour over the oil mixture. If cheese is not completely covered, pour on more oil. Leave, covered, overnight in the refrigerator. Drain the cheese and place in a hinged wire rack. Grill the cheese over hot coals until light golden brown and just beginning to melt. Drain and dry the vine leaves. Wash the radicchio and break apart the leaves. Arrange radicchio and endive leaves on 4 small plates and place a vine leaf on top. Place the

cooked cheese on top of the vine leaf and spoon some of the oil mixutre over each serving.

Gorgonzola and Bean Salad with Pine Nuts

PREPARATION TIME: 20 minutes

COOKING TIME: 4-5 minutes

SERVES: 4 people

12oz green beans, ends trimmed
½ cup pine nuts, toasted if desired
1 cup crumbled gorgonzola or other blue
  cheese
2 tbsps red wine vinegar
6 tbsps olive oil
½ clove garlic, finely minced
Salt and pepper
2 heads radicchio

This page: Cheese and Vine Leaves. Facing page: Gorgonzola and Bean Salad with Pine Nuts (top), and Spinach Salad with Bacon, Hazelnuts and Mushrooms (bottom).

If the beans are large, cut across in half or thirds. Place in boiling salted water and cook for 4-5 minutes or until tender-crisp. Rinse under cold water and leave to drain. Toast pine nuts, if desired, at 350°F (180°C), for 10 minutes. Allow to cool. Mix the vinegar, oil, garlic, salt and pepper until well emulsified. Toss the beans in the dressing and add the cheese and nuts. Separate the leaves of radicchio, wash and dry. Arrange on salad plates and spoon the bean salad on top. Alternatively, tear radicchio into bite-size pieces and toss all the ingredients together.

Beet and Celeriac Salad

PREPARATION TIME: 25 minutes

COOKING TIME: 20 minutes

SERVES: 4 people

1 large celeriac root, peeled
4-6 cooked beets
4 green onions chopped
Juice of ½ a lemon

DRESSING
1½ cups sour cream
2 tsps white wine vinegar
Pinch sugar
2 tsps celery seed
1½ tbsps parsley

Cut the celeriac into ½ inch dice. Cook in boiling salted water with the juice of half a lemon for about 20 minutes or until tender. Drain and set aside to cool. Dice the beets the same size as the celeriac. Mix the beets with the green onions and carefully combine with the celeriac. Mix the dressing ingredients together, reserving half of the parsley. Combine the dressing with the celeriac and the beets, taking care not to over mix. Sprinkle the remaining parsley over the salad before serving.

Parsley Salad Vinaigrette

PREPARATION TIME: 20 minutes

COOKING TIME: 2 minutes

SERVES: 4 people

2 large bunches parsley (preferably flat Italian variety)
8oz tomatoes, quartered and seeded
1 cup stoned black olives, sliced
½ cup vegetable oil
1 clove garlic, finely minced
3 tbsps white wine vinegar
1 tsp dry mustard
Pinch sugar
Salt and pepper
½ cup grated fresh Parmesan cheese

Pick over the parsley and discard any yellow and thick stems. Break parsley into individual leaves. Cut the

This page: **Red Cabbage, Celery and Carrot Salad. Facing page: Parsley Salad Vinaigrette (top), and Beet and Celeriac Salad (bottom).**

tomatoes into ½ inch dice. Use 2 tbsps of measured oil and heat in a small frying pan. Add the finely chopped garlic and cook slowly to brown lightly. Combine with the remaining oil, vinegar, mustard, sugar, salt and pepper and beat well. Toss the dressing with the parsley, tomatoes and olives before serving. Sprinkle over the Parmesan cheese.

Red Cabbage, Celery and Carrot Salad

PREPARATION TIME: 15 minutes

SERVES: 6-8 people

1 small head red cabbage
4-6 carrots, peeled
4-6 sticks celery

DRESSING
½ cup oil
1 tbsp white wine vinegar
2 tbsps lemon juice
1 tbsp honey
1 tbsp celery seed
2 tsps chopped parsley
Salt and pepper

Cut the cabbage in quarters and remove the core. Grate coarsely or

slice finely. Grate the carrots coarsely. Cut the celery into very fine strips. Combine all the vegetables in a large salad bowl or in individual bowls. Mix the salad dressing ingredients very well. This can be done by hand with wire whisk or in a blender. Once the dressing is well emulsified, add the celery seeds and whisk again. Pour over the salad and toss before serving.

Three Bean Salad

PREPARATION TIME: 15 minutes plus marinating time

SERVES: 6-8 people

1 8oz can chickpeas
1 8oz can red kidney beans
1 8oz can green flageolet beans
6-8 tomatoes, quartered

DRESSING
½ cup olive oil and vegetable oil mixed
4 tbsps white wine vinegar
2 tbsps chopped parsley
1 tbsp chopped basil
1 shallot, finely chopped
1 clove garlic, finely minced
Salt and pepper

Drain and rinse all the beans. Mix the dressing ingredients together thoroughly and combine with the beans. Allow to marinate for 2 hours. Mound the beans into a serving dish and surround with the quartered tomatoes to serve.

Pea, Cheese and Bacon Salad

PREPARATION TIME: 20 minutes

COOKING TIME: 15-20 minutes

SERVES: 6 people

6 strips bacon, rind and bones removed
1lb fresh or frozen shelled peas
4oz Colby cheese
4 sticks celery, diced
4 green onions, sliced thinly or 1 small red onion, diced
1 red pepper, cored, seeded and diced

1 head Buttercrunch lettuce
¾ cup sour cream or natural yogurt
1 tbsp chopped fresh mixed herbs
1 tsp white wine vinegar
1 tsp sugar
Salt and pepper

Dice the bacon and cook gently in a small frying pan until the fat runs. Turn up the heat and fry the bacon until brown and crisp. Remove to paper towels to drain. Meanwhile cook the peas in boiling salted water for 15-20 minutes for fresh peas and 5 minutes for frozen peas. When the peas are cooked, drain and refresh under cold water and leave to drain dry. Cut the cheese into dice slightly larger than the peas. Dice the celery and red pepper to the same size as the cheese. Combine the peas,

This page: Tomato and Mozzarella Salad with Fresh Basil. Facing page: Three Bean Salad (left), and Pea, Cheese and Bacon Salad (right).

cheese, celery, green onions, red pepper and bacon in a bowl. Mix the dressing ingredients together, reserving half of the chopped mixed herbs. Combine the vegetables and bacon with half of the dressing. Separate the leaves of the lettuce and wash well. Pat dry and arrange on serving dishes. Spoon on the salad mixture and top with the remaining dressing. Sprinkle the reserved chopped herbs on top of the dressing.

Tomato and Mozzarella Salad with Fresh Basil

PREPARATION TIME: 15 minutes

SERVES: 4 people

3 large beefsteak tomatoes, sliced ¼ inch thick
6oz mozzarella cheese, drained, dried and sliced ¼ inch thick
4 tbsps coarsely chopped fresh basil leaves

DRESSING
6 tbsps olive oil and vegetable oil mixed
2 tbsps balsamic vinegar or white wine vinegar
¼ tsp Dijon mustard
Salt and pepper

GARNISH
Fresh basil leaves

Arrange the tomato slices and mozzarella cheese slices in overlapping circles on four individual salad plates. Sprinkle the fresh chopped basil leaves on top and garnish in the center with the whole basil leaves. Mix all the dressing ingredients together very well and spoon some over the salads before serving. Serve the rest of the dressing separately.

Cracked Wheat Salad

PREPARATION TIME: 20 minutes

SERVES: 4-6 people

2 cups bulgur wheat, washed and drained
4 green onions, chopped
1 cucumber, cut in small cubes
Juice and rind of 1 lemon
4 tomatoes, cubed
4 sticks celery, diced
½ cup toasted sunflower seeds
1 cup crumbled feta cheese
½ cup olive oil
1 clove garlic, minced
Salt and pepper
4 tbsps chopped mixed herbs

Place the washed bulgur wheat in clean water and leave to soak for 5 minutes. Drain and squeeze as much moisture out as possible. Spread the wheat out onto a clean towel to drain and dry. When the wheat is dry put into a large bowl with all the remaining ingredients and toss together carefully so that the cheese does not break up. Allow the salad to chill for up to 1 hour before serving. If desired, garnish the salad with whole sprigs of herbs.

Spinach Salad with Bacon, Hazelnuts and Mushrooms

PREPARATION TIME: 20 minutes

COOKING TIME: 2-3 minutes

SERVES: 4 people

1½ lbs spinach, stalks removed, washed and dried
6 strips bacon, bones and rind removed
8oz mushrooms, sliced
1 cup hazelnuts, roasted, skinned and roughly chopped

DRESSING
½ cup oil
3 tbsps white wine vinegar
1 tsp Dijon mustard
1 shallot, finely chopped
Salt and pepper
Pinch sugar (optional)

Tear the spinach leaves into bite-size pieces and put into a serving bowl. Fry or broil the bacon until brown and crisp. Crumble the bacon and sprinkle over the spinach. Add the hazelnuts and mushrooms to the spinach salad and toss. Mix all the dressing ingredients very well and pour over the salad just before serving.

Cucumber and Mint Salad

PREPARATION TIME: 30 minutes

SERVES: 4 people

1 large or 2 small cucumbers, peeled for a striped effect or scratched with the prongs of a fork lengthwise along the skin
Salt

DRESSING
1 cup sour cream or natural yogurt
2 tbsps chopped fresh mint
1 tbsp chopped parsley
Pinch sugar
Squeeze lemon juice
Salt and pepper

GARNISH
Whole sprigs of mint

Slice the cucumber thinly in rounds. Place the cucumber in a colander and sprinkle lightly with salt. Leave for 30 minutes to drain. Rinse the cucumber under cold water to remove the salt and pat dry. Mix the sour cream or yogurt with the sugar, lemon juice, salt, pepper, mint and parsley. Pour over the drained cucumber and toss. Leave refrigerated for 30 minutes before serving, and garnish with whole sprigs of mint.

Potato Salad with Mustard-Chive Dressing

PREPARATION TIME: 25 minutes

COOKING TIME: 20 minutes

SERVES: 6 people

3lbs potatoes, new or red variety
6 sticks celery, thinly sliced
1 red pepper, seeded, cored and diced
3 hard-boiled eggs

DRESSING
1 cup prepared mayonnaise
1 cup natural yogurt
4 tbsps Dijon mustard and mild mustard mixed half and half
1 bunch chives, snipped
Salt and pepper

Facing page: Cucumber and Mint Salad (top), and Cracked Wheat Salad (bottom).

Cook the potatoes in their skins for about 20 minutes in salted water. When the potatoes are tender, drain and peel while still warm. Cut the potatoes into cubes and mix with the celery and red pepper. Set the potato salad aside to cool while mixing the dressing. Combine the mayonnaise, yogurt, mustard, half the chives, salt and pepper and mix well. Toss carefully with the potato salad so that the potatoes do not break up. Spoon the salad into a serving dish and slice the hard-boiled eggs into rounds, or chop roughly. Arrange the hard-boiled eggs in circles on top of the potato salad or scatter over, if chopped. Sprinkle over reserved chives and refrigerate for about 1 hour before serving.

Red, Green and Yellow Pepper Salad

PREPARATION TIME: 20 minutes

SERVES: 6 people

3 sweet red peppers
3 green peppers
3 yellow peppers
Oil
½ cup small black olives, stoned
2 tbsps finely chopped coriander leaves
3 hard-boiled eggs

DRESSING
6 tbsps oil
2 tsps lemon juice
2 tbsps white wine vinegar
1 small clove garlic, finely minced
Pinch salt
Pinch cayenne pepper
Pinch sugar (optional)

Cut all the peppers in half and remove the seeds and cores. Press lightly with palm to flatten. Brush the skin side of each pepper with oil and place under a preheated broiler about 6 inches from the heat. Cook until the skin chars. Remove and wrap the peppers in a clean towel. Leave them to cool 10-15 minutes. Mix the dressing ingredients and quarter the eggs. Unwrap the peppers and peel off the skin. Cut the peppers into strips about 1 inch wide and arrange

in a circle, alternating colors. Arrange the olives and quartered egg in the center. Sprinkle the coriander leaves over the peppers and spoon over the dressing. Leave the salad, covered, in the refrigerator for 1 hour before serving. Peeled peppers will keep covered in oil up to 5 days in the refrigerator.

Coleslaw

PREPARATION TIME: 25 minutes

SERVES: 6 people

DRESSING
1 cup prepared mayonnaise
4 green onions finely chopped
1 cup sour cream
2oz Roquefort or blue cheese

This page: Zanzibar Shrimp. Facing page: Coleslaw (top), and Potato Salad with Mustard-Chive Dressing (bottom).

¼ tsp Worcestershire sauce
1 tsp vinegar
2 tbsps chopped parsley
Pinch sugar
Salt and pepper

SALAD
1 medium size head white cabbage, shredded
6 carrots, peeled and coarsely grated
1 green pepper, cut into thin short strips
1 cup roasted peanuts or raisins

Combine all the dressing ingredients,

reserving half the parsley, and refrigerate in a covered bowl for about 1 hour to allow the flavors to blend. Combine the dressing with the salad ingredients and toss to serve. Sprinkle on reserved chopped parsley.

Zanzibar Shrimp

PREPARATION TIME: 25 minutes

COOKING TIME: 18-23 minutes

SERVES: 4 people

1lb jumbo shrimp, shelled and de-veined
1 large fresh pineapple, peeled, cored and
    cut into chunks
Oil

SAUCE
½ cup orange juice
1 tbsp vinegar
1 tbsp lime juice
1 tsp dry mustard
1 tbsp brown sugar
Remaining pineapple

GARNISH
Flaked coconut
Curly endive

Thread the shrimp and pineapple pieces on skewers, alternating each ingredient. Use about 4 pineapple pieces per skewer. Place the remaining pineapple and the sauce ingredients into a food processor and purée. Pour into a small pan and cook over low heat for about 10-15 minutes to reduce slightly. Place the kebabs on a lightly oiled rack above the coals and cook about 6 minutes, basting frequently with the sauce. Sprinkle cooked kebabs with coconut and serve on endive leaves. Serve remaining sauce separately.

Egg Mayonnaise with Asparagus and Caviar

PREPARATION TIME: 25 minutes

COOKING TIME: 10 minutes

SERVES: 4-6 people

12 asparagus spears, trimmed and peeled
6 hard-boiled eggs
1½ cups prepared mayonnaise
1 tbsp lemon juice
Hot water
Red caviar

Tie asparagus in a bundle and cook in a deep saucepan of boiling salted water, keeping the asparagus tips out of the water. The tips will cook in the steam and the thick stalks will cook in the water, thus helping the asparagus to cook evenly. Cook about 5-8 minutes or until just tender. Rinse under cold water and drain. Meanwhile, place eggs in

This page: **Red, Green and Yellow Pepper Salad. Facing page: Egg Mayonnaise with Asparagus and Caviar.**

boiling water. Bring water back to the boil and cook eggs for 10 minutes. Cool completely under cold running water and peel. Combine mayonnaise and lemon juice. If very thick, add enough hot water until of coating consistency. Arrange eggs cut side down on a plate and coat with the mayonnaise. Surround with asparagus and garnish the eggs with caviar.

THE COOKOUT COOKBOOK

MEAT AND POULTRY

Kashmiri Lamb Kebabs

PREPARATION TIME: 20 minutes

COOKING TIME: 10 minutes

SERVES: 4 people

1½ lbs lamb shoulder or leg
2 tbsps oil
1 clove garlic, finely minced
1 tbsp ground cumin
1 tsp turmeric
1 tsp grated fresh ginger
Chopped fresh coriander or parsley leaves
Salt and pepper
1 red pepper, cut in 1 inch pieces
1 small onion, cut in rings

Cut the lamb in 1 inch cubes. Heat the oil and cook the garlic, cumin, turmeric and ginger for 1 minute. Add the coriander, salt and pepper. Allow to cool and then rub the spice mixture over the meat. Leave covered in the refrigerator for several hours. Thread the meat on skewers, alternating with the pepper slices. Cook about 10 minutes, turning frequently. During the last 5 minutes of cooking, thread sliced onion rings around the meat and continue cooking until the onion is cooked and slightly browned and meat has reached desired doneness.

Ground Lamb Kebabs with Olives and Tomatoes

PREPARATION TIME: 20 minutes

COOKING TIME: 10 minutes

SERVES: 4 people

4 tbsps bulgur wheat, soaked and drained

1¼ lbs ground lamb
1 clove garlic, finely minced
2 tsps ground cumin
Pinch cinnamon
Salt and pepper
1 egg, beaten
Oil
16 large green olives, stoned
16 cherry tomatoes

This page: Mustard Grilled Pork with Poppy Seeds. Facing page: Kashmiri Lamb Kebabs (left) and Ground Lamb Kebabs with Olives and Tomatoes (right).

SAUCE
1 cup yogurt
2 tbsps chopped fresh mint
Salt and pepper

Soak the bulgur wheat until soft.
Wring out and spread on paper
towels to drain and dry. Mix with the
remaining ingredients and enough of
the beaten egg to bind together. The
mixture should not be too wet. Form
into small balls about 1½ inches in
diameter. Thread onto skewers with
the olives and tomatoes. Brush with
oil and grill about 10 minutes,
turning frequently. Mix the yogurt,
mint, salt and pepper and serve with
the kebabs.

Mustard Grilled Pork with Poppy Seeds

PREPARATION TIME: 20 minutes
plus marinating time

COOKING TIME: 45 minutes to
1 hour

SERVES: 4-6 people

4 6-7oz pieces whole pork tenderloin
2 tbsps black poppy seeds

MARINADE
1 tbsp mild mustard
4 tbsps oil
4 tbsps unsweetened apple juice
1 clove garlic, finely minced
Salt and pepper

SWEET MUSTARD SAUCE
1 cup mild mustard
¼ cup brown sugar
¼ cup dry cider or unsweetened apple juice
2 tsps chopped fresh or crumbled dried tarragon
Pinch cayenne pepper
Salt

Mix the marinade and rub into the
pork. Place the pork in a dish or pan
and cover. Refrigerate for 4 hours or
overnight. Using a grill with an
adjustable rack, place the pork over
the coals on the highest level or set
an electric or gas grill to a medium
temperature. Cook the pork for

45 minutes-1 hour, basting with the
marinade and turning frequently.
Lower the shelf or raise the
temperature. Baste frequently with
the sauce during the last 10 minutes
of cooking time. During the last
5 minutes, sprinkle the pork with the
poppy seeds. Serve the pork sliced
thinly with the remaining sauce.

Turkey and Pancetta Rolls

PREPARATION TIME: 30 minutes

COOKING TIME: 20-30 minutes

SERVES: 4-6 people

2 turkey breasts, 1lb each, skinned
⅓ cup butter softened
1 clove garlic, minced
1 tbsp oregano leaves
16 slices pancetta or prosciutto ham
Salt and pepper
Oil

Cut the turkey breasts in half,
lengthwise. Place each piece between
two sheets of plastic wrap and bat
out each piece with a rolling pin or
meat mallet to flatten. Mix the butter,
garlic, oregano, salt and pepper
together. Spread half of the mixture
over each slice of turkey. Lay 4 slices
of pancetta on top of each piece of
turkey. Roll up, tucking in the sides
and tie with fine string in 3 places.
Spread the remaining butter on the
outside of each roll. Cook the rolls
over medium-hot coals until tender.
Insert a meat thermometer into each
roll to check doneness. The
temperature should read 190°F
(90°C). Cooking should take
approximately 20-30 minutes. Slice
each roll into ½ inch rounds to serve.

Niçoise Chicken

PREPARATION TIME: 30 minutes

COOKING TIME: 20 minutes

SERVES: 4 people

4 boned chicken breasts, unskinned
4 tbsps oil
2 tbsps lemon juice

TAPENADE FILLING
1lb large black olives, stoned
2 tbsps capers
1 clove garlic, peeled and roughly chopped
4 anchovy fillets
2 tbsps olive oil
Raw tomato sauce

1lb ripe tomatoes, peeled, seeded and chopped
1 shallot, very finely chopped
2 tbsps chopped parsley
2 tbsps chopped basil
2 tbsps white wine vinegar
2 tbsps olive oil
1 tbsp sugar
Salt and pepper
1 tbsp tomato paste (optional)

Cut a pocket in the thickest side of
the chicken breasts. Combine half
the olives, half the capers and the
remaining ingredients for the
tapenade in a blender or food
processor. Work to a purée. Add the
remaining olives and capers and
process a few times to chop them
roughly. Fill the chicken breasts with
the tapenade. Chill to help filling to
firm. Baste the skin side with oil and
lemon juice mixed together. Cook
skin side down first for 10 minutes
over medium hot coals. Turn over,
baste again and grill for another
10 minutes on the other side.
Meanwhile, combine the sauce
ingredients and mix very well. Serve
with the chicken.

Orange Grilled Duck with Sesame and Spice

PREPARATION TIME: 20 minutes
plus marinating time

COOKING TIME: 40 minutes

SERVES: 4 people

4 boned duck breasts
4 tbsps sesame seeds

**Facing page: Turkey and Pancetta
Rolls (top) and Niçoise Chicken
(bottom).**

minutes before the duck is cooked, sprinkle the orange slices with brown sugar and grill on both sides to glaze. Serve with the duck.

Herb and Onion Grilled Lamb Chops

PREPARATION TIME: 10 minutes

COOKING TIME: 15 minutes

SERVES: 4 people

4 leg chops, cut ¾ inch thick

MARINADE
1 large onion, finely chopped
1 tbsp parsley, finely chopped
1 tbsp fresh thyme or mint leaves, roughly chopped
2 fresh bay leaves, cut in thin shreds with scissors
1 clove garlic, finely minced
3 tbsps oil
Juice of ½ lemon
Salt and pepper

Combine all the marinade ingredients and pour over the chops in a dish. Leave, covered, 2 hours in the refrigerator. Place on a rack over hot coals and cook the chops 15 minutes, turning often and basting frequently with the remaining marinade.

Barbecued Flank Steak

PREPARATION TIME: 25 minutes

COOKING TIME: 45-55 minutes

SERVES: 6 people

3½ lbs flank steak, in one piece

BARBECUE SEASONING
4 tbsps salt
1½ tsps freshly ground pepper
1½ tsps cayenne pepper (or paprika for a milder tasting mixture)

This page: Orange Grilled Duck with Sesame and Spice. Facing page: Herb and Onion Grilled Lamb Chops (top), and Barbecued Flank Steak (bottom).

MARINADE
4 tbsps soy sauce
½ cup dry white wine
3 tbsps oil
Pinch ground nutmeg
Pinch ground ginger
Pinch ground mustard
Salt and pepper

SAUCE
Reserved marinade
¾ cup orange juice
1 shallot, finely chopped
2 tsps cornstarch

GARNISH
1 orange, peeled and thinly sliced in rounds
Brown sugar

Score the fat side of each duck breast with a sharp knife. Mix the marinade ingredients together and pour over the duck in a shallow dish. Cover and refrigerate for 2 hours. Turn the duck frequently. Place the duck breasts fat side down on grill. Cook for 20 minutes per side, basting frequently. If the duck appears to be cooking too quickly, turn more often. Combine the sauce ingredients and add any remaining marinade. Cook 1-2 minutes over moderate heat until boiling and, just before the duck is finished cooking, brush the fat side lightly with the sauce and sprinkle on the sesame seeds. Turn fat side down onto the grill for 1 minute. Serve remaining sauce with the duck. Five

Barbecued Ribs

PREPARATION TIME: 15 minutes

COOKING TIME: 2 hours

SERVES: 4-6 people

2-3 racks pork spare ribs (about 5lbs)
Barbecue sauce (see recipe for Barbecued
  Flank Steak)
or
Sweet mustard sauce (see recipe for
  Mustard Grilled Pork with Poppy
  Seeds)

Leave the ribs in whole racks. Combine the ingredients for either sauce and pour over the meat in a roasting pan. Cover with foil and bake, turning and basting frequently, for 1 hour in a 325°F (150°C) oven. Uncover and bake 30 minutes more in the oven. Finish on a barbecue grill over moderately hot coals for about 30 minutes, basting frequently with the sauce. Cut between the bones into pieces. Serve with the remaining sauce.

Javanese Pork

PREPARATION TIME: 20 minutes

COOKING TIME: 30-45 minutes

SERVES: 4 people

4 pork rib or loin chops cut 1 inch thick
4 tbsps dark soy sauce
Large pinch cayenne pepper
3 tbsps lime or lemon juice
1 tbsp ground coriander
2 tbsps oil
2 tbsps brown sugar
4 medium-sized sweet red peppers
Oil
1 bunch fresh coriander

Snip the fat around the edges of the chops at ½ inch intervals to prevent curling. Mix soy sauce, cayenne pepper, lemon juice, coriander and oil together in a dish or pan. Place the pork chops in the marinade and leave, covered, in the refrigerator for

This page: Javanese Pork. Facing page: Chinese Pork and Eggplant Kebabs (left), and Barbecued Ribs (right).

BARBECUE SAUCE
4 tbsps oil
1¼ cups tomato ketchup
3 tbsps Worcestershire sauce
6 tbsps cider vinegar
4 tbsps soft brown sugar
4 tbsps chopped onion
1 clove garlic, crushed (optional)
1 bay leaf
4 tbsps water
2 tsps dry mustard
Dash tabasco
Salt and pepper

First prepare the barbecue sauce. Combine all the ingredients, reserving salt and pepper to add later. Cook in a heavy saucepan over low heat for 30 minutes, stirring frequently and adding more water if the sauce reduces too quickly.

Remove the bay leaf and add salt and pepper to taste before using. The sauce should be thick. Use the sauce for basting while cooking, or serve hot to accompany cooked meat and poultry. Score the meat across both sides with a large knife. Mix together the barbecue seasoning and rub 2 tbsps over the meat, reserving the rest of the seasoning for other use. Sear the meat on both sides over hot coals. Raise the grill rack or lower the temperature on a gas or electric grill. Baste with the sauce and grill the meat slowly. During last 5 minutes, lower the rack or raise the temperature and grill the meat quickly on both sides, basting with the sauce. Slice the meat thinly across the grain and serve with any remaining sauce.

**This page: Stuffed Hamburgers.
Facing page: Butterflied Lamb.**

1 hour. Turn over after 30 minutes. Place on grill over medium hot coals or on a middle rack. Mix sugar into remaining marinade. Cook chops for 15-20 minutes on each side until well done. Baste with the marinade frequently during the last 10-15 minutes of cooking. Meanwhile, wash and dry the peppers and brush with oil on all sides. Place alongside pork for half of its cooking time. Turn the peppers often. They will soften and char on the outside. Serve the pork chops with peppers, and garnish with coriander leaves.

Butterflied Lamb

PREPARATION TIME: 30 minutes plus marinating time
COOKING TIME: 40-50 minutes
SERVES: 6-8 people

*4lbs leg of lamb
5 tbsps oil
Juice and rind of one lemon
Small bunch mint, roughly chopped
Salt and coarsely ground black pepper
1 clove garlic, crushed*

To butterfly the lamb, cut through the skin along the line of the main bone down to the bone. Cut the meat away from the bone, opening out the leg while scraping against the bone with a small, sharp knife. Take out the bone and remove excess fat. Flatten thick places by batting with a rolling pin or meat mallet.

Alternatively, make shallow cuts halfway through the thickest parts and press open. Thread two or three long skewers through the meat – this will make the meat easier to handle and turn on the grill. Place in a plastic bag or large, shallow dish. Mix the other ingredients together and pour over the lamb, rubbing it in well. Cover the dish or seal the bag and leave at room temperature for 6 hours or overnight in the refrigerator. Turn the lamb frequently. Remove from the dish or the bag and reserve the marinade. Grill on the skin side first, at least 6 inches away from the coals. Grill 20 minutes per side for pink lamb and 30-40 minutes per side for more well done lamb. Baste frequently during grilling. Remove the skewers and cut the slices across the grain. If fresh mint is unavailable, use rosemary, fresh or dried. Alternatively, roast lamb in a 350°F (180°C) oven for half of the cooking time and grill for the last half of cooking.

Stuffed Hamburgers

PREPARATION TIME: 30 minutes
COOKING TIME: 20 minutes
SERVES: 4-8 people

*2lbs ground beef
1 onion, finely chopped
4 tbsps Worcestershire sauce
Salt and pepper
8 hamburger buns*

GUACAMOLE BURGERS

FILLING
*4oz Monterey Jack cheese, cubed
1 mild chili pepper, thinly sliced and seeds
   removed*

TOPPING
*1 avocado, peeled and mashed
1 small clove garlic, crushed
2 tsps lemon or lime juice
1 tomato, peeled, seeded and finely
   chopped
Salt and pepper*

BLUE CHEESE BURGERS
FILLING
*4oz blue cheese, crumbled
¼ cup chopped walnuts*

TOPPING
1 tbsp steak sauce
5 tbsps prepared mayonnaise
6 tbsps sour cream or yogurt
Salt and pepper

GRUYÈRE AND MUSHROOM BURGERS

FILLING
2oz mushrooms, roughly chopped
4oz Gruyère or Swiss cheese, cubed

TOPPING
1lb tomatoes
1 clove garlic, finely minced
2 tbsps tarragon, chopped
1 tbsp tarragon vinegar
Pinch sugar
2 tbsps oil
Salt and pepper

Mix the hamburger ingredients well, mold the meat around the chosen fillings and press carefully into patties. Mix the guacamole topping ingredients together and set aside while grilling the hamburgers. Mix the topping for the blue cheese burgers and refrigerate until needed. For the Gruyère burger topping, roughly chop tomatoes and then finely chop in a blender or food processor. Sieve to remove the seeds and skin, combine with the remaining tomato sauce ingredients and mix well. Grill hamburgers over hot coals 10 minutes per side. Quickly grill cut sides of the hamburger buns to heat through and place the hamburgers inside. Spoon on the appropriate toppings for each filling.

Chicken Tikka

PREPARATION TIME: 20 minutes
COOKING TIME: 10-15 minutes
SERVES: 4 people

3lb chicken, skinned and boned

MARINADE
½ cup natural yogurt
1 small piece ginger, grated
1 clove garlic, finely minced
1 tsp chili powder, hot or mild

½ tsp ground coriander
½ tsp ground cumin
¼ tsp turmeric
¼ tsp red food coloring (optional)
Juice of one lime
Salt and pepper

Half head Iceberg lettuce, shredded
4 lemon wedges
4 small tomatoes, quartered

Cut chicken into 1 inch pieces. Mix all the marinade ingredients together. Pour over the chicken and stir well. Cover and leave for several hours in the refrigerator. Thread chicken on skewers and grill 10-15 minutes, turning frequently. Baste with any remaining marinade. Serve on a bed of shredded lettuce with tomatoes and lemon wedges.

Indian Chicken

PREPARATION TIME: 15 minutes plus marinating time
COOKING TIME: 45 minutes to 1 hour
SERVES: 4-6 people

3lbs chicken, cut into 8 pieces
2 cups natural yogurt
2 tsps ground coriander
2 tsps paprika
1 tsp ground turmeric
Juice of 1 lime
1 tbsp honey
½ clove garlic, finely minced
1 small piece ginger, peeled and grated

Pierce the chicken all over with a fork or skewer. Combine all the remaining ingredients and spread half the mixture over the chicken, rubbing in well. Place the chicken in a shallow dish or a plastic bag and cover or tie and leave for at last 4 hours or overnight in the refrigerator. If your barbecue has adjustable shelves, place on the level furthest from the coals. Arrange the chicken skin side down and grill until lightly browned, turn over and cook again until lightly browned. Baste frequently with remaining marinade. Lower the grill for the last 15 minutes and cook, turning and basting frequently, until the chicken is brown and the skin is

crisp. Alternatively, cook the chicken in a covered pan in the oven at 325°F (150°C) for 45 minutes to 1 hour and grill for the last 15 minutes for flavor and color. Serve any remaining yogurt mixture separately as a sauce.

Chinese Pork and Eggplant Kebabs

PREPARATION TIME: 20 minutes
COOKING TIME: 15-20 minutes
SERVES: 4 people

1lb pork tenderloin, cut in 1 inch cubes
2 medium onions, cut in 1 inch pieces
1 large eggplant, cut in 1½ inch cubes
2 tbsps hoisin sauce
3 tbsps soy sauce
4 tbsps rice wine or dry sherry
1 clove garlic, finely minced
Sesame seeds
Salt

Sprinkle the eggplant cubes with salt and leave in a colander to drain for 30 minutes. Rinse well and pat dry. Pre-cook in 2 tbsps oil to soften slightly. Thread the pork, onion and eggplant on skewers, alternating the ingredients. Mix the hoisin sauce, soy sauce, rice wine or sherry and garlic together. Brush the kebabs with the mixture and place them on a lightly-oiled grill. Cook about 15-20 minutes, turning and basting frequently. During the last 2 minutes sprinkle all sides with sesame seeds and continue grilling to brown the seeds. Pour over any remaining sauce before serving.

Facing page: Indian Chicken (top), and Chicken Tikka (bottom).

Burgundy Beef Kebabs

PREPARATION TIME: 20 minutes plus marinating time

COOKING TIME: 10 minutes

SERVES: 4 people

4oz shallots or button onions, parboiled 3 minutes and peeled
1½ lbs sirloin or butt steak, cut in 1 inch thick cubes

MARINADE
1 cup burgundy or other dry red wine
3 tbsps oil
1 bay leaf
1 clove garlic, peeled
1 sliced onion
6 black peppercorns
1 sprig fresh thyme
Pinch salt

SAUCE
1 cup sour cream
2 tbsps chopped fresh mixed herbs (such as parsley, thyme, marjoram and chervil)
1 tbsp red wine vinegar
Pinch sugar
2 tsps Dijon mustard
Salt and pepper

Bring the marinade ingredients to the boil in a small saucepan. Remove from the heat and allow to cool completely. When cold, pour over the meat in a plastic bag. Seal the bag well, but place it in a bowl to catch any drips. Marinate overnight in the refrigerator, turning the bag occasionally. Thread the meat onto skewers with the onions and grill 10 minutes, turning and basting frequently. Mix the sauce ingredients together and serve with the kebabs.

Smoked Sausage and Apple Kebabs

PREPARATION TIME: 20 minutes

COOKING TIME: 6 minutes

SERVES: 4 people

Two rings smoked pork or beef sausage, cut in 1 inch thick slices

4 small apples, quartered and cored
8 sage leaves
Lemon juice
Quarter quantity sweet mustard sauce (see recipe for Mustard Grilled Pork with Poppy Seeds)

Brush the apples with lemon juice. Thread onto skewers, alternating with sausage pieces and bay leaves.

Brush with the mustard sauce and grill 10 minutes, turning frequently and basting with the sauce. Serve any remaining sauce with the kebabs if desired.

Ham and Apricot Kebabs

PREPARATION TIME: 15 minutes

COOKING TIME: 12 minutes

SERVES: 4 people

1½ lbs cooked ham cut in 2 inch cubes
8oz canned or fresh apricots, halved and
    stoned
1 green pepper, cut in 2 inch pieces

APRICOT BASTE
¾ cup light brown sugar
4 tbsps apricot jam, sieved
6 tbsps wine or cider vinegar
1 tsp dry mustard
3 tbsps light soy sauce
Salt and pepper

Thread ham, apricots and pepper
pieces onto skewers, alternating the
ingredients. Mix the apricot baste
ingredients together and cook over
gentle heat to dissolve the sugar.
Brush over kebabs as they cook. Turn
and baste several times, grilling for
about 12 minutes over hot coals. If
using canned apricots, reserve the
juice and add to any baste that
remains after the kebabs are cooked.
Bring this mixture to the boil to
reduce slightly and serve as a sauce
with the kebabs.

Spicy Madeira Steaks

PREPARATION TIME: 20 minutes

COOKING TIME: 15 minutes

SERVES: 4 people

4 butt steaks about 6oz each

MARINADE
4 tbsps oil
½ cup ketchup
¾ cup red wine vinegar
1 clove garlic, crushed
1 tsp pepper
1 tsp ground cloves
½ tsp cinnamon
½ tsp thyme leaves

SAUCE
½ cup reserved marinade
2 tbsps flour
½ cup beef stock
½ cup Madeira
Salt

Combine marinade ingredients and

pour over steaks in a dish. Cover and
refrigerate at least 4 hours. Remove
from marinade and place over hot
coals. Grill, basting frequently, until
of desired doneness. Combine flour
with reserved marinade, beating well
to mix to a smooth paste. Gradually
beat in stock. Bring to the boil in a
small saucepan, stirring constantly.
Cook until thickened, about

1 minute. Reduce heat and simmer
5 minutes. Stir in Madeira and add
salt to taste. Serve with the steak.

**Facing page: Spicy Madeira Steaks
(left), and Burgundy Beef Kebabs
(right). This page: Ham and
Apricot Kebabs (left), and Smoked
Sausage and Apple Kebabs (right).**

FISH AND SEAFOOD

Marsala Fish

PREPARATION TIME:	25 minutes
COOKING TIME:	10-15 minutes
SERVES:	4 people

4 medium sized mackerel, trout or similar
  fish
Juice of 1 lemon
2 tsps turmeric
2 green chili peppers, finely chopped
1 small piece ginger, grated
1 clove garlic, finely minced
Pinch ground cinnamon
Pinch ground cloves
4 tbsps oil
Salt and pepper
Fresh coriander leaves

ACCOMPANIMENT
½ cucumber, finely diced
½ cup thick natural yogurt
1 green onion, finely chopped
Salt and pepper

Clean and gut the fish. Cut three slits
on each side of the fish. Combine
spices, lemon juice, oil, garlic and
chili peppers and spread over the fish
and inside the cuts. Place whole
sprigs of coriander inside the fish.
Brush the grill rack lightly with oil or
use a wire fish rack. Cook the fish
10-15 minutes, turning often and
basting with any remaining mixture.
Combine the accompaniment
ingredients and serve with the fish.

Scallops, Bacon and Shrimp Kebabs

PREPARATION TIME:	25 minutes
COOKING TIME:	20-25 minutes
SERVES:	4 people

12 large, raw scallops
12 raw jumbo shrimp, peeled and de-
  veined
12 slices smoked bacon
Juice of 1 lemon
2 tbsps oil
Coarsely ground black pepper

**This page: Scallops, Bacon and
Shrimp Kebabs. Facing page:
Marsala Fish.**

RED CHILI YOGURT SAUCE
2 cloves garlic, finely chopped
1 red pepper, grilled and peeled
1 red chili pepper, chopped
3 slices bread, crusts removed, soaked in
*   water*
3 tbsps olive oil
½ cup natural yogurt

Wrap each scallop in a slice of bacon and thread onto skewers, alternating with shrimp. Mix the lemon juice, oil and pepper and brush over the shellfish as they cook. Turn frequently and cook until the bacon is lightly crisped and the scallops are just firm. Meanwhile, prepare the sauce. Squeeze the bread to remove the water and place the bread in a blender. Add the finely chopped garlic, the chopped red chili pepper and peeled red pepper and blend well. With the machine running, pour in the oil through the funnel in a thin, steady stream. Keep the machine running until the mixture is a smooth, shiny paste. Combine with the yogurt and mix well. Serve with kebabs.

Grilled Sardines with Lemon and Oregano

PREPARATION TIME: 15 minutes

COOKING TIME: 6-8 minutes

SERVES: 4-6 people

8-12 fresh sardines, gutted, scaled, washed
*   and dried*
8-12 sprigs fresh oregano
⅓ cup olive oil
Juice and rind of 2 lemons
Salt and pepper
1 tbsp dried oregano

Place one sprig of oregano inside each fish. Mix oil, lemon juice and rind, salt and pepper together. Make two slits on each side of the fish. Brush the fish with the lemon mixture and grill over hot coals for 3-4 minutes per side, basting frequently. When the fish are nearly done, sprinkle the dried oregano on the coals. The smoke will give the fish extra flavor. May be served as a appetizer or main course.

Gray Mullet with Fennel

PREPARATION TIME: 15 minutes

COOKING TIME: 18-22 minutes

SERVES: 4 people

2-4 gray mullet, depending upon size,
*   gutted and cleaned*

MARINADE
⅓ cup oil
1 tbsp fennel seeds, slightly crushed
1 clove garlic, finely minced
Juice and rind of one lemon
2 tbsps chopped fennel tops
Salt and pepper

Heat oil and add the fennel seeds. Cook for one minute. Add the garlic and remaining ingredients except the fennel tops. Leave the mixture to cool completely. Pour over the fish in a shallow dish. Cover and refrigerate for 1 hour. Grill over hot coals 10-12 minutes per side. Sprinkle over fennel tops halfway through cooking. Tops may also be placed directly on the coals for aromatic smoke.

Swordfish Steaks with Green Peppercorns and Garlic Oregano Sauce

PREPARATION TIME: 25 minutes

COOKING TIME: 15 minutes

SERVES: 4 people

2 tbsps fresh green peppercorns (substitute
*   well-rinsed canned green peppercorns)*
6 tbsps lemon juice
4 tbsps olive oil
Salt
4 swordfish steaks (tuna steaks may also
*   be used)*

SAUCE
1 egg
1 clove garlic, roughly chopped
½ cup oil
1 tbsp lemon juice
2 sprigs fresh oregano
Salt and pepper

Crush the green peppercorns slightly

and mix with lemon juice, oil and salt. Place the swordfish steaks in a shallow dish and pour over the lemon oil mixture. Cover and refrigerate several hours, turning frequently. Process the egg and garlic in a blender or food processor. With the machine running, pour oil through the funnel in a thin, steady stream. When the sauce is thick, strip the leaves off the oregano and process to chop them finely. Add lemon juice, salt and pepper. Grill the swordfish over hot coals for 15 minutes, basting frequently and turning once. Serve with the sauce. (Peppercorns will pop when exposed to the heat of the grill.)

Grilled Red Mullet with Tarragon

PREPARATION TIME: 15 minutes

COOKING TIME: 10-16 minutes

SERVES: 4 people

4 large or 8 small red mullet, gutted,
*   scaled, washed and dried*
4 or 8 sprigs fresh tarragon

MARINADE
4 tbsps oil
2 tbsps tarragon vinegar
Salt and pepper

SAUCE
1 egg
½ cup oil
1 tsp Dijon mustard
1 tbsp chopped tarragon
1 tbsp chopped parsley
1 tbsp tarragon vinegar
2 tbsps heavy cream
1 tsp brandy
Salt and pepper

Place a sprig of tarragon inside each fish. Cut two slits on the side of each fish. Mix the marinade ingredients together, pour over the fish in a shallow dish and refrigerate for 30

Facing page: Swordfish Steaks with Green Peppercorns and Garlic Oregano Sauce (top), and Grilled Sardines with Lemon and Oregano (bottom).

minutes, covered. Put the egg in a blender or food processor. Add the mustard, salt and pepper and process to mix. Add the oil through the funnel, with the machine running, in a thin, steady stream. When all the oil has been added, add the herbs, vinegar and brandy and process to mix well. Fold in the heavy cream and pour into a serving dish. Keep in the refrigerator until ready to use. Cook the fish for 5-8 minutes per side, depending upon size of fish. Baste frequently with the marinade while cooking. Serve with the sauce.

This page: Gray Mullet with Fennel (top), and Grilled Red Mullet with Tarragon (bottom). Facing page: Monkfish and Pepper Kebabs with Bernaise Butter Sauce.

Monkfish and Pepper Kebabs with Bernaise Butter Sauce

PREPARATION TIME: 30 minutes
COOKING TIME: 25 minutes
SERVES: 4 people

1lb monkfish, cut into 2 inch pieces
8 strips bacon, rind and bone removed
2 pieces lemon grass
1 green pepper, cut in 2 inch pieces
1 red pepper, cut in 2 inch pieces
12 mushroom caps
8 bay leaves
Oil

BERNAISE BUTTER SAUCE
½ cup dry white wine
4 tbsps tarragon vinegar
2 shallots, finely chopped
1 tbsp chopped fresh tarragon
1 tbsp chopped fresh chervil or parsley
1 cup butter, softened

Salt and pepper

Cut the bacon in half lengthwise and again in half across. Peel the lemon grass and use only the core. Cut into small pieces. Place a piece of fish on each strip of bacon and top with a piece of lemon grass. Roll up. Thread the rolls of fish on skewers, alternating with peppers, mushrooms and bay leaves. Brush with oil and grill 15 minutes, turning and basting often. While the fish cooks, heat the white wine, vinegar and shallots in a small saucepan until boiling. Cook rapidly to reduce by half. Add the herbs and lower the heat. Beat in the softened butter a bit at a time until the sauce is the thickness of hollandaise sauce. Season with salt and pepper to taste and serve with the fish kebabs.

BARBECUED VEGETABLES

Grilled Fennel

PREPARATION TIME: 15 minutes

COOKING TIME: 20 minutes

SERVES: 4 people

4 small bulbs fennel
Juice and rind of 1 lemon
4 tbsps oil
1 shallot, finely chopped
Salt and pepper

Remove the fennel tops and reserve them. Cut the fennel bulbs in half and remove the cores. Parboil the fennel for 5 minutes. Combine the juice and rind of the lemon, salt, pepper, oil and shallot. Pour over the fennel and set aside for 15 minutes. Place the fennel bulbs on hot coals and cook 15 minutes, turning often and brushing with the lemon mixture. Chop the fennel tops finely and sprinkle over the grilled fennel. Pour over any remaining lemon juice mixture to serve.

Grilled Tomatoes

PREPARATION TIME: 15 minutes

COOKING TIME: 6 minutes

SERVES: 4 people

4 beefsteak tomatoes cut in half
1 tbsp oregano, fresh or dried
2 tbsps olive oil
1 tbsp lemon juice
Salt and pepper
4oz feta cheese, crumbled

Mix the oil, lemon juice, salt, pepper and oregano together. Brush over the cut side of the tomatoes and grill that side first for 3 minutes over hot coals. Brush the skin side of the tomatoes and turn them over. Grill 3 minutes more on skin side and remove the tomatoes to a serving dish. Sprinkle over the crumbled feta cheese and pour over the remaining basting mixture to serve.

Grilled Corn-on-the-Cob

PREPARATION TIME: 20 minutes

COOKING TIME: 15 minutes

SERVES: 4 people

4 large ears of corn, husks and silk
  removed, parboiled 5 minutes
½ cup butter, melted
Salt and pepper
Chili powder or paprika (optional)

Brush the drained corn liberally with melted butter. Sprinkle with salt and pepper. Chili powder or paprika can be substituted for the pepper, if desired. Grill over medium hot coals for 15 minutes, turning often and basting frequently with butter. To serve, pour over any remaining butter.

Grilled Eggplant

PREPARATION TIME: 30 minutes

COOKING TIME: 20-24 minutes

SERVES: 4 people

2 eggplants
¾ cup olive oil
6 tbsps lemon juice
1 tbsp cumin seed
1 clove garlic, finely chopped
2 tbsps parsley, chopped
Salt and pepper

Cut the eggplant into rounds about 1 inch thick. Score the surface of each round lightly with a sharp knife, sprinkle with salt and leave to stand for 30 minutes. Heat oil for 1 minute and add the cumin seed and cook for the 30 seconds. Add the garlic and cook for a further 30 seconds. Add the lemon juice. Rinse the salt from the eggplant slices and pat dry. Brush one side of the slices with the basting mixture. Grill on a lightly oiled rack or place in a hinged wire rack. Cook for 10-12 minutes per side until soft, basting frequently. Place the slices in a serving dish and pour over the remaining basting mixture. Sprinkle with parsley just before serving.

Grilled Mushrooms

PREPARATION TIME: 10 minutes

COOKING TIME: 15-20 minutes

SERVES: 4 people

1lb large mushrooms, cleaned

MARINADE
1 tbsp chopped tarragon, fresh or dried
Grated rind and juice of 1 orange
1 tbsp tarragon vinegar
2 tbsps oil
Salt and pepper

Mix together the marinade

Facing page: Grilled Tomatoes (top), and Grilled Fennel (bottom).

ingredients. Cut the stalks from the mushrooms and place the mushroom caps in a shallow dish. Pour over the marinade and leave the mushrooms for 15-20 minutes. Place the mushrooms in a wire rack and cook 15-20 minutes over hot coals. Brush the mushrooms frequently with the marinade and turn them once or twice. Remove to a serving dish and pour over the remaining marinade to serve.

Zucchini, Pepper and Onion Kebabs

PREPARATION TIME: 20 minutes

COOKING TIME: 10-12 minutes

SERVES: 4 people

4-6 zucchini, ends trimmed
1 large onion
1 large green pepper
1 large red pepper
Oil
4 tbsps dry white wine
1 tsp thyme
2 tsps chopped parsley
1 tsp chopped chives
½ cup melted butter

Peel the zucchini with swivel peeler for a striped effect. Parboil 4 minutes. Refresh under cold water. Cut in 2 inch pieces. Quarter the onion and cut in large pieces, separating the layers. Cut the peppers in half and remove the core and seeds. Cut into pieces the same size as the onion. Thread the vegetables onto skewers. Melt the butter and add the wine and cook 1 minute. Add the herbs, salt and pepper. Brush the kebabs lightly with oil and grill 5-6 minutes per side. Brush frequently with the butter mixture. When the zucchini are tender, remove to a serving dish. Pour over the remaining butter.

Barbecued Baked Potatoes

PREPARATION TIME: 15 minutes

COOKING TIME: 25 minutes

SERVES: 4-6 people

4 large potatoes, scrubbed but not peeled
Salt and pepper
Paprika
½ cup melted butter

SAUCE
1 cup sour cream
2 tsps red wine vinegar

This page: Zucchini, Pepper and Onion Kebabs. Facing page: Grilled Eggplant and Grilled Mushrooms.

SALADS WITH FRUIT

Waldorf Salad

PREPARATION TIME: 20 minutes

SERVES: 6 people

4 sticks celery, diced
4 apples, mixture of red-skinned and
    green-skinned, diced
6oz grapes, black and white, halved and
    seeded
1 cup walnuts or pecans, roughly chopped
1 cup prepared mayonnaise
4 tbsps heavy cream
Juice of half a lemon

Mix the celery, apples, grapes and
nuts together and toss with the
lemon juice. Lightly whip the cream
and fold into the mayonnaise. Fold
the dressing into the salad and serve
chilled. If desired, substitute raisins
for the grapes and garnish with
2 tbsps chopped parsley.

Fruit Salad with Coconut Cream Dressing

PREPARATION TIME: 30 minutes

SERVES: 6-8 people

2lb fresh assorted fruit, such as:
Pineapple, peeled, cored and cut in
    wedges
Melon, skinned and sliced
Bananas, peeled, cut in thick rounds and
    sprinkled with lemon juice
Apricots, halved and stoned and sprinkled
    with lemon juice
Peaches, peeled and sliced and sprinkled
    with lemon juice
Strawberries, hulled and washed
Raspberries or blackberries, washed
Papaya, peeled and sliced

Currants, stems removed
Blueberries, washed
Kiwi, peeled and sliced
Kumquats, thinly sliced, seeds removed
Fresh figs, quartered
Pears, peeled, cored and sliced

DRESSING
1 cup natural yogurt
½ cup coconut cream
2-3 tbsps lime juice
Seeds of 1 fresh pomegranate

Arrange assortment of fruit on
plates. Mix together the ingredients
for the dressing and drizzle over the
fruit. Sprinkle on the pomegranate
seeds.

Green and Gold Sunflower Salad

PREPARATION TIME: 15 minutes

SERVES: 4 people

2 large ripe avocados
8 ripe apricots

DRESSING
3 tbsps sunflower oil
1 tbsp lemon juice
Salt and pepper

YOGURT DRESSING
½ cup natural yogurt
2 tsps honey
Grated rind of 1 lemon
2 tsps chopped parsley
4 tbsps toasted sunflower seeds
1 small Buttercrunch lettuce, washed and
    separated into leaves

Prepare the oil and lemon juice
dressing. Cut avocados in half and
remove the stones. Peel and cut into

slices. Cut apricots in half and
remove the stones. If the apricots are
large, cut in half again. Add the
apricots to the avocados, spooning
over the dressing. Mix all the
ingredients for the yogurt dressing
together except the sunflower seeds.
Place the lettuce leaves on salad
plates and arrange the avocado and
apricots on top. Spoon over some of
the yogurt dressing and sprinkle the
sunflower seeds onto the dressing.
Serve immediately and hand extra
dressing separately.

Watercress and Orange Salad

PREPARATION TIME: 20 minutes

SERVES: 4-6 people

3 large bunches watercress, well washed
    and thick stalks removed
4 oranges, peeled and segmented

DRESSING
6 tbsps vegetable oil
Juice and rind of 1 orange
Pinch sugar
Squeeze lemon juice
Salt and pepper

Break watercress into small sprigs
and discard any yellow leaves.
Arrange the watercress with the
orange segments on plates or toss in
one large salad bowl. Mix the
dressing ingredients together very
well and pour over the salad just
before serving.

**Facing page: Watercress and
Orange Salad (top), and Waldorf
Salad (bottom).**

Fennel, Orange and Tomato Salad

PREPARATION TIME: 25 minutes

COOKING TIME: 3-4 minutes

SERVES: 4 people

2 bulbs fennel, green top trimmed and
    reserved
2 large, ripe tomatoes
2 oranges

DRESSING
2 tbsps orange juice
1½ tbsps lemon juice
Zest of 1 orange
⅓ cup olive oil and vegetable oil mixed
    half and half
1 tsp chopped fresh oregano or basil

Pinch sugar
Salt and pepper

Choose fennel with a lot of feathery green top. Reserve the tops. Cut the cores out of the bottom of the fennel bulbs and discard. Bring water to the boil in a large saucepan. Slice the fennel thinly, lengthwise, and place the slices in the boiling water. Cook until translucent and slightly softened, about 3-4 minutes. Carefully remove the slices to a colander and rinse under cold water. Leave to drain. Place the tomatoes into the boiling water for 5-10 seconds. Put immediately into cold water. Peel and slice into ¼ inch rounds. Grate or use a zester to remove the peel from 1 orange. Peel

This page: Fruit Salad with Coconut Cream Dressing. Facing page: Green and Gold Sunflower Salad (top), and Fennel, Orange and Tomato Salad (bottom).

off the pith with knife and peel the remaining orange. Slice both oranges into ¼ inch rounds. Prepare the dressing by whisking all the ingredients very well and reserving the orange zest. Arrange the fennel, tomato and orange slices in circles on a round serving dish. Pour over the dressing and sprinkle on the orange zest. Chop the fennel tops and sprinkle over or use whole to garnish the salad.

THE COOKOUT COOKBOOK

INDEX